To Mom
Love Rhonda

Contents

Isaiah's Prophecy	Isaiah 7:14
For Unto Us A Child Is Born	Isaiah 9:26
Holy Night	Luke 2:8-14
The Story of the Wise Men	Matthew 2:1-12
The Heavens Declare	Psalm 19:12, 14
Be Ye Therefore Perfect	Matthew 5:48
The Lord Is My Shepherd	Psalm 23
Ask, Seek, Knock	Matthew 7:7-11
I Do Set My Bow	Genesis 9:13
The Golden Rule	Matthew 7:12
Of Such Is The Kingdom	Mark 10:14-16
The Ten Commandments	Exodus 20:3-17
Blessed Is The Man	Psalm 1
The Word	John 1:1-5, 14
Be Still	Psalm 46:10
Faith, Hope, Charity	1 Corinthians 13:1-13
The Lordship of God	Psalm 24
Time	Ecclesiastes 3:1-8
Give Thanks	Psalm 136:1-9, 26
The Lord's Prayer	Matthew 6:9-13
Seek Ye The Lord	Isaiah 55:6-7
Holy, Holy, Holy	Habakkuk 2:20

Thus it is written

editor
van b. hooper

Biblical Scrolls

of passages
engrossed
and
illuminated
by

Kate K. Ball

Isaiah's Prophecy

The ancient writings of the prophet Isaiah, in the eighth century B.C., predicted the birth of Christ.

Even as the parchment scrolls were unrolled to reveal his written testimony, so were truths of Scripture unfolded.

Isaiah's prophecy, addressed to "the House of David," came out of the dark days of oppression with a bright promise of a Messiah. Out of the dim past came Isaiah's prophecy of an approaching miracle.

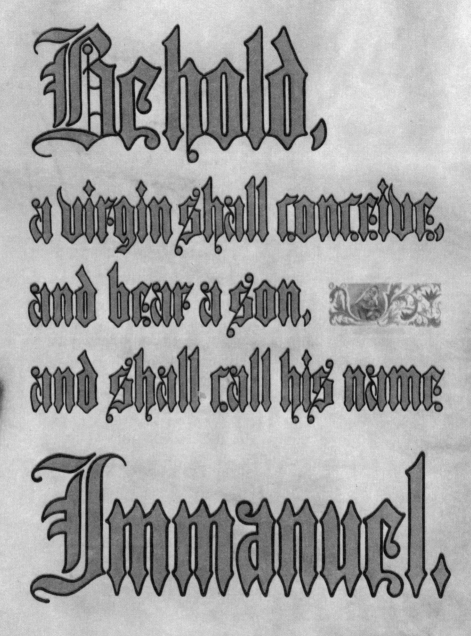

Behold,
a virgin shall conceive,
and bear a son,
and shall call his name
Immanuel.

Isaiah 7:14

For Unto Us A Child Is Born

Christ fulfilled every promise prophesied by Isaiah and during His lifetime added descriptive, easily understood titles to those of the prophet.

The meaningful decoration on the scroll expresses the Cup of Salvation, the Bread of Life, the Fruit of the Harvest, the Rose of Sharon, the Good Shepherd, the Lamp, the Shining Star, the Word, the Sheltering Wings, the Branch, the King, the Strong Tower, and the Dove of Peace.

The people that walked in darkness have seen a great light; they that dwell in the land of the shadow of death, upon them hath the light shined.

For unto us a child is born, unto us a son is given: and the government shall be upon his shoulder: and his name shall be called

Wonderful,

Counsellor,

The mighty God,

The everlasting Father,

The Prince of Peace.

Isaiah 9:2,6

ENGROSSED AND ILLUMINATED BY KATE KRAUSE BALL FOR THE GLORY OF OUR LORD IN THE YEAR 1955

Holy Night

The world's sweetest story, the manger scene, shows the baby Jesus with Mary the mother, and Joseph.

It is nighttime with the light inside the stable, radiating from the Christ Child. Lambs are the symbol of Jesus, the "Lamb of God," who was sacrificed for the world. Doves represent the spirit of God. The open doorway indicates that the Child belongs to the world and was never shut away from it.

In the pastoral scene, an angel makes the announcement to the frightened shepherds, while above them appears a Heavenly Host.

This is the story of the announcement to the shepherds of the birth of Christ. The scroll is without gold for the birth of Jesus was humble.

Holy Night

And there were in the same country shepherds abiding in the field, keeping watch over their flock by night.

And, lo, the angel of the Lord came upon them, and the glory of the Lord shone round about them: and they were sore afraid.

And the angel said unto them, Fear not: for, behold I bring you good tidings of great joy, which shall be to all people.

For unto you is born this day in the city of David a Saviour, which is Christ the Lord.

And this shall be a sign unto you: Ye shall find the babe wrapped in swaddling clothes, lying in a manger.

And suddenly there was with the angel a multitude of the heavenly host praising God, and saying,

Glory to God in the highest, and on earth peace, good will toward men.

Luke 2: 8-14

The Story of the Wise Men

In contrast to the humble shepherds who went to the Babe in the manger, the Wise Men, who sought the Child, were rulers of men, with wealth, knowledge, and power. They recognized the meaning of the star and believed in its prophesy. In wisdom, they followed it to bring gifts to the greater King.

The scroll is designed with dignity and richness. Mystery surrounds the kings from the faraway lands.

The star is the five-pointed star of Christianity expressive of man with head uplifted, two arms outstretched, and two feet upon the ground.

The Story of the

Wise Men

Now when Jesus was born in Bethlehem of Judaea in the days of Herod the king, behold, there came wise men from the east to Jerusalem,

Saying, Where is he that is born King of the Jews? for we have seen his star in the east, and are come to worship him. ___

When Herod the king had heard these things, he was troubled, and all Jerusalem with him. ___

And when he had gathered all the chief priests and scribes of the people together, he demanded of them where Christ should be born. ___

And they said unto him, In Bethlehem of Judaea: for thus it is written by the prophet, ___

And thou Bethlehem, in the land of Juda, art not the least among the princes of Juda: for out of thee shall come a Governor, that shall rule my people of Israel. ___

Then Herod, when he had privily called the wise men, enquired of them diligently what time the star appeared. ___

And he sent them to Bethlehem, and said, Go and search diligently for the young child; and when ye have found him, bring me word again, that I may come and worship him also. ___

When they had heard the king, they departed; and, lo, the star, which they saw in the east, went before them, till it came and stood over where the young child was. ___

When they saw the star, they rejoiced with exceeding great joy.

And when they were come into the house, they saw the young child with Mary his mother, and fell down, and worshipped him: and when they had opened their treasures, they presented him gifts; gold, and frankincense, and myrrh. ___

And being warned of God in a dream that they should not return to Herod, they departed into their own country another way. ___

Matthew 2: 1-12

ENGROSSED BY KATE KRAUSE BALL IN THE YEAR OF OUR LORD 1950 AND FOR HIS GLORY

The Heavens Declare the Glory

The grandeur of the heavens testifies to God as the Creator, and is a continuous witness to His glory.

The Psalmist recognizes that man is forgetful. Acknowledging the Lord as his strength and Savior, he prays to follow in God's way.

The heavens declare the glory of God; and the firmament sheweth his handywork.

Day unto day uttereth speech, and night unto night sheweth knowledge.

✴

Let the words of my mouth, and the meditation of my heart, be acceptable in thy sight, O Lord, my strength, and my redeemer. ✴

Psalm 19: 1, 2, and 14

Be Ye Therefore Perfect

As the tree is bent so shall the tree grow. Elect to be perfect and you shall be perfect. The will of man in this world determines the man-to-be in the next world. Here life is conceived and takes shape and reaches fulfillment. As no perfection is attained here, so no imperfection exists in Heaven. A life patterned after the Master, shall become like unto the Master.

Be ye therefore perfect, — even as your Father which is in heaven is perfect.

Matthew 5:48

ENGROSSED BY KATE KRAUSE BALL FOR THE GLORY OF THE LORD IN THE YEAR 1957

The Lord Is My Shepherd

This scroll, expressing the shepherd's care of the sheep, places the lamb in first importance.

At the very center of the design is the shepherd's comforting rod and staff. Around them are grouped the green pastures and still waters, the horn with the healing oil, and the cup that runneth over.

The design leads upward to the light which gives strength to the one who is traveling through the valley of the shadow.

The floral ornament, the oxalis, represents the clover of the field as it is known in the Holy Land.

23rd Psalm

A Psalm of David

1. The Lord is my shepherd; I shall not want.

2. He maketh me to lie down in green pastures: he leadeth me beside the still waters.

3. He restoreth my soul: he leadeth me in the paths of righteousness for his name's sake.

4. Yea, though I walk through the valley of the shadow of death, I will fear no evil: for thou art with me; thy rod and thy staff they comfort me.

5. Thou preparest a table before me in the presence of mine enemies: thou anointest my head with oil; my cup runneth over.

6. Surely goodness and mercy shall follow me all the days of my life: and I will dwell in the house of the Lord forever.

Ask, Seek, Knock

This is an expression of parental love with greater promise than any earthly father could give. Yet the child who expects all things from his father may place little confidence in the heavenly Father whom he does not see. He becomes another doubting Thomas. Yet he must know that God's promises are just as real as his own father's promises.

Ask, Seek, Knock,

Ask, and it shall be given you;

Seek, and ye shall find;

Knock, and it shall be opened unto you:

*For every one that asketh receiveth;
and he that seeketh findeth;
to him that knocketh it shall be opened.*

Or what man is there of you, whom if his son ask bread, will he give him a stone?

Or if he ask a fish, will he give him a serpent?

If ye then, being evil, know how to give good gifts unto your children, how much more shall your Father which is in heaven give good things to them that ask him?

Matthew 7:7-11

ENGROSSED BY KATE KRAUSE BALL FOR THE GLORY OF OUR LORD IN THE YEAR 1957

I Do Set My Bow

There was a promise, a pledge, given by God to man. It was expressed to Noah in words. It has been repeated to every generation in the rainbow, a token of the covenant between God and man.

I do set my bow in the cloud, and it shall be for a token of a covenant between me and the earth. Genesis 9:13

The Golden Rule

The Golden Rule carries a broad meaning of friendship among men the world around. Men of different color, different nationality, different ages, and different walks of life, are neighbors.

The practice of the Golden Rule results in benefits expressed by "Peace with God," "Peace with fellowman," and "Peace with oneself." With peace, we realize development in industry, education, literature, science, art, music, the comforts of home and the plentiful fruits of labor.

The ivy for decoration is appropriate as a symbol of that which will hold fast and endure.

Three drops of blood, a tragic warning, are shown which result when the Golden Rule is opposed.

The wording on the scroll is the Golden Rule as it used to be taught: the word, "as" substituted for the word "whatsoever" expresses not only the deed, but the manner of doing one to another.

The

Golden Rule

As ye would that men should do unto you — do ye even so unto them.

Matthew 7:12

Peace with God

Peace with fellowman

Peace with oneself

Industry · Education · Literature · Science · Art · Music · Play · Contentment · Plenty

ENGROSSED BY KATE KRAUSE BALL · FOR THE GLORY OF OUR LORD · IN THE YEAR 1944

Of Such Is The Kingdom of God

Little children of all nations, innocent of evil, trusting, believing, hoping, and ready to love, are very dear in the sight of God.

Jesus taught that we are children of God, and should come to the Father in the spirit of the little ones.

*S*uffer the little children to come unto me, and forbid them not: for

# of such is the kingdom of God

*V*erily I say unto you,

Whosoever shall not receive the kingdom of God

as a little child, he shall not enter therein.

And he took them up

in his arms, put his hands upon them, and

blessed them.

St. Mark 10: 14, 15, 16

The Ten Commandments

The scroll for the Ten Commandments has the circle and the square as the chief design. The circle, symbolizing eternity, and the square, symbolizing truth, combine to mean Eternal Truth.

As the Ten Commandments were given to Moses, it is fitting that the decoration be in the manner of the mosaic art.

The plan of the scroll is simple, direct, almost severe; quite appropriate for the Ten Commandments.

The Ten Commandments

Exodus 20: 3 – 17

1. Thou shalt have no other Gods before me.

2. Thou shalt not make unto thee any graven image or any likeness of anything that is in heaven above, or that is in the earth beneath, or that is in the water under the earth. Thou shalt not bow down thyself to them, nor serve them: for I the Lord thy God am a jealous God visiting the iniquity of the fathers upon the children unto the third and fourth generation of them that hate me, And shewing mercy unto thousands of them that love me and keep my commandments.

3. Thou shalt not take the name of the Lord thy God in vain; for the Lord will not hold him guiltless that taketh his name in vain.

4. Remember the sabbath day to keep it holy. Six days shalt thou labour, and do all thy work: But the seventh day is the sabbath of the Lord thy God: in it thou shalt not do any work, thou, nor thy son, nor thy daughter, nor thy man-servant, nor thy maidservant, nor thy stranger that is within thy gates: For in six days the Lord made heaven and earth, the sea, and all that in them is, and rested the seventh day: wherefore the Lord blessed the sabbath day and hallowed it.

5. Honour thy father and thy mother: that thy days may be long upon the land which the Lord thy God giveth thee.

6. Thou shalt not kill.

7. Thou shalt not commit adultery.

8. Thou shalt not steal.

9. Thou shalt not bear false witness against thy neighbour.

10. Thou shalt not covet thy neighbour's house, thou shalt not covet thy neighbour's wife, nor his manservant, nor his maidservant, nor his ox, nor his ass, nor anything that is thy neighbour's.

Blessed Is the Man

The fig tree, native of the Holy Land, is the decorative motif used for Psalm 1.

The Psalm, first song of David, describes the two paths which a man may follow. One is fruitful, the other barren. One knows gain, the other loss. The promise of one is life, the other death. Blessedness, the knowledge of God, the recognition by God, and the joy of Heaven is the rich reward of the godly.

PSALM 1.

Blessed is the man that walketh not in the counsel of the ungodly, nor standeth in the way of sinners, nor sitteth in the seat of the scornful.

But his delight is in the law of the Lord; and in his law doth he meditate day and night.

And he shall be like a tree planted by the rivers of water, that bringeth forth his fruit in his season; his leaf also shall not wither; and whatsoever he doeth shall prosper.

The ungodly are not so, but are like the chaff which the wind driveth away.

Therefore, the ungodly shall not stand in the judgement, nor sinners in the congregation of the righteous.

For the Lord knoweth the way of the righteous: but the way of the ungodly shall perish.

The Word

The majesty and splendor of the heavens, the light of the stars, the blue of the firmament, and the royal hues of purple illustrate appropriately the Word.

The Word

1 In the beginning was the Word, and the Word was with God, and the Word was God.

2 The same was in the beginning with God.

3 All things were made by him; and without him was not any thing made that was made.

4 In him was life; and the life was the light of men.

5 And the light shineth in the darkness; and the darkness comprehended it not.

14 And the Word was made flesh, and dwelt among us, (and we beheld his glory, the glory as of the only begotten of the Father,) full of grace and truth.   St. John 1 : 1 ~ 5, 14

ENGROSSED BY KATE KRAUSE BALL FOR THE GLORY OF OUR LORD IN THE YEAR 1959

Be Still

The Psalmist invites a pause to be silent, and realize that this is God's world.

"Alpha and Omega" in the continuous form of the circle, show that God's love, care and dominion is without beginning and without end, encompassing at all times.

The rays of light and the stars further show that "Thine is the kingdom, and the power, and the glory forever."

Faith, Hope, Charity

This is the measure of the heart. Faith, hope, and charity (love) are qualities that make character— things which are felt rather than seen. The scriptural passage conveys the thought of great beauty.

So, the artist, using abstract form, has represented these qualities with color — violet for faith, rose for hope, and blue for charity. Each color has its own beauty, and each is harmonious with the others.

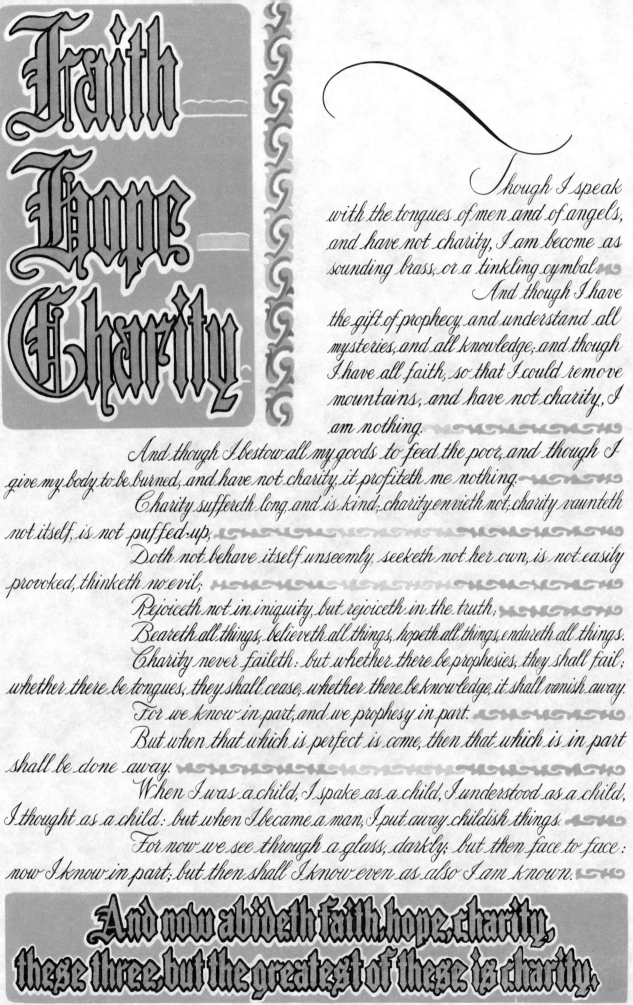

Faith Hope Charity

Though I speak with the tongues of men and of angels, and have not charity, I am become as sounding brass, or a tinkling cymbal.

And though I have the gift of prophecy, and understand all mysteries, and all knowledge; and though I have all faith, so that I could remove mountains, and have not charity, I am nothing.

And though I bestow all my goods to feed the poor, and though I give my body to be burned, and have not charity, it profiteth me nothing.

Charity suffereth long, and is kind; charity envieth not; charity vaunteth not itself, is not puffed up,

Doth not behave itself unseemly, seeketh not her own, is not easily provoked, thinketh no evil;

Rejoiceth not in iniquity, but rejoiceth in the truth;

Beareth all things, believeth all things, hopeth all things, endureth all things.

Charity never faileth: but whether there be prophesies, they shall fail; whether there be tongues, they shall cease; whether there be knowledge, it shall vanish away.

For we know in part, and we prophesy in part.

But when that which is perfect is come, then that which is in part shall be done away.

When I was a child, I spake as a child, I understood as a child, I thought as a child: but when I became a man, I put away childish things.

For now we see through a glass, darkly; but then face to face: now I know in part; but then shall I know even as also I am known.

And now abideth faith, hope, charity, these three but the greatest of these is charity.

1 Corinthians 13:1-13

The Lordship of God

The glories of the earth, the beauty of God's handiwork, the admonition of the Lord that to receive His blessings — clean hands and a pure heart are required of thee.

Psalm 24

The Lordship of God

The earth is the Lord's, and the fulness thereof; the world, and they that dwell therein.

For he hath founded it upon the seas, and established it upon the floods.

Who shall ascend into the hill of the Lord? or who shall stand in his holy place?

He that hath clean hands and a pure heart; who hath not lifted up his soul unto vanity, nor sworn deceitfully.

He shall receive the blessing from the Lord, and righteousness from the God of his salvation.

This is the generation of them that seek him, that seek thy face, O Jacob. Selah.

Lift up your heads, O ye gates; and be ye lift up, ye everlasting doors; and the King of glory shall come in.

Who is this King of glory? The Lord strong and mighty, the Lord mighty in battle.

Lift up your heads, O ye gates; even lift them up, ye everlasting doors; and the King of glory shall come in.

Who is this King of glory? The Lord of hosts, he is the King of glory. Selah.

ENGROSSED BY KATE KRAUSE BALL FOR THE GLORY OF OUR LORD IN THE YEAR 1960

Time

Riches, health, talents, and opportunities are not equally divided among men, but the gift of time is the same to all. The most powerful man on earth cannot be granted an extra hour in the day.

God who gives the tree a season for growth, blossom, fruit and rest, gives to man sufficient time for every purpose. Time cannot be purchased, sold, stored up, nor cast away. It may bring glory; it may bring shame. But in the end it will serve God's purpose.

Time

To every thing there is a season, and a time to every purpose under the heaven:

A time to be born, and a time to die: a time to plant, and a time to pluck up that which is planted;

A time to kill, and a time to heal; a time to break down, and a time to build up;

A time to weep, and a time to laugh; a time to mourn, and a time to dance;

A time to cast away stones, and a time to gather stones together; a time to embrace, and a time to refrain from embracing;

A time to get, and a time to lose; a time to keep, and a time to cast away;

A time to rend, and a time to sew; a time to keep silence, and a time to speak;

A time to love, and a time to hate; a time of war, and a time of peace.

Ecclesiastes 3:1-8

ENGROSSED BY KATE KRAUSE BALL FOR THE GLORY OF OUR LORD IN THE YEAR 1956

Give Thanks

Thanks often repeated are easy to express, and if
we attempted to give thanks for every good gift,
our words would become a never-ending chant.

Give Thanks

O give thanks unto the Lord for he is good:

for his mercy endureth forever.

O give thanks unto the God of gods:

for his mercy endureth forever.

O give thanks to the Lord of lords:

for his mercy endureth forever.

To him who alone doeth great wonders:

for his mercy endureth forever.

To him that by wisdom made the heavens:

for his mercy endureth forever.

To him that stretched out the earth above the waters:

for his mercy endureth forever.

To him that made great lights:

for his mercy endureth forever.

The sun to rule by day:

for his mercy endureth forever.

The moon and stars to rule by night:

for his mercy endureth forever.

O give thanks unto the God of heaven:

for his mercy endureth forever.

Psalm 136:1-9,26

ENGROSSED BY KATE KRAUSE BALL FOR THE GLORY OF OUR LORD IN THE YEAR 1957   1958 © K.K.B.

The Lord's Prayer

The symbolic decoration in this scroll represents Heaven and earth, things spiritual and things temporal.

The upper part of the design, symbolizing Heaven, shows the hand of God in the position of bestowing a blessing. It emerges from a triangle, symbol of the Holy Trinity. Behind this triangle are three circles. Three symbolizes the Trinity; the circle, eternity; together they mean the Everlasting Trinity.

Royalty and power are expressed by purple in the triangle; yellow speaks of light.

The dove at each side of the design represents the Spirit of God descending in answer to prayer.

The lower part of the design is indicative of earthly things. Hands are lifted in petition.

The abundance of fruit is an expression of God's goodness. Wheat, symbol of the bread of life, represents God's provision for man's physical needs. The lamb is the emblem of Jesus, Son of God, sent as His proof of His love for the children of earth, His perfect answer to man's prayer.

The Lord's Prayer

🌿 Our Father which art in heaven, Hallowed be thy name.

🌿 Thy kingdom come. Thy will be done in earth, as it is in heaven.

🌿 Give us this day our daily bread.

🌿 And forgive us our debts, as we forgive our debtors.

🌿 And lead us not into temptation but deliver us from evil: For thine is the kingdom, and the power, and the glory, forever. Amen. Matthew 6: 9-13

Seek Ye the Lord

As spring returns to the earth and blossoms forth into the radiance of the day, so does the prophet call for a return to the Lord, leaving behind wicked thoughts and ways.

Isaiah 55:6,7 Seek ye the Lord while he may be found, call ye upon him while he is near:

Let the wicked forsake his way and the unrighteous man his thoughts and let him return unto the Lord, and he will have mercy upon him; and to our God, for he will abundantly pardon.

Engrossed and illuminated by Kate Krause Ball for the glory of our Lord in the year 1959

Holy, Holy, Holy

Above, beyond, and within the furrowed earth, God is. In silence we listen and hear His voice.